Reading/Writing Companion

mheducation.com/prek-12

Copyright © 2023 McGraw Hill

Send all inquiries to:
McGraw Hill
1325 Avenue of the Americas
New York, NY 10019

ISBN: 978-1-26-572675-1
MHID: 1-26-572675-2

Printed in the United States of America.

5 6 7 8 9 LMN 26 25 24 23 22

A

Welcome to WONDERS!

We are so excited about how much you will learn and grow this year! We're here to help you set goals for your learning.

You will build on what you already know and learn new things every day.

You will read a lot of fun stories and interesting texts on different topics.

You will write about the texts you read. You will also write texts of your own. You will do research as well.

You will explore new ideas by reading different texts.

Each week, we will set goals on the My Goals page. Here is an example:

I can read and understand texts.

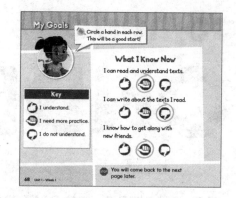

As you read and write, you will learn skills and strategies to help you reach your goals.

You will think about your learning and sometimes circle a hand to show your progress.

Here are some questions you can ask yourself.

- Did I understand the task?

- Was it easy?

- Was it hard?

- What made it hard?

It is okay if I need more practice. The most important thing is to do my best and keep learning!

If you need more help, you can choose what to do.

- Talk to a friend or teacher.
- Use an Anchor Chart.
- Choose a center activity.

At the end of each week, you will complete a fun task to show what you have learned.

Then you will return to your My Goals page and think about your learning.

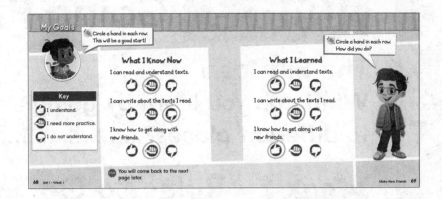

I learned so much about reading and understanding texts. I started with a sideways thumb, and now I circled the thumbs up for that goal!

Let's get started!

Unit 3 Going Places

The Big Idea

Week 1 • Rules to Go By

Literature Big Book *How Do Dinosaurs Go to School?*

Shared Read "Can I Pat It?"

Paired Selection "Be Safe!"

Shared Read "Tim Can Tip It"

Digital Tools Find this eBook and other resources at: my.mheducation.com

2

Week 2 • Sounds Around Us

Danielle D. Hughson/Moment/Getty Images

Week 3 • The Places We Go

Going Places

The Big Idea

What can you learn by going to different places?

- Talk about the places in the picture. Take turns talking with your partner.

- Circle the places you go to where you live.

Build Knowledge

? Essential Question What rules do we follow in different places?

Build Vocabulary

 Talk about rules we follow in different places. What words tell about different rules?

 Draw a picture of one of the words.

 Write the word.

Ariel Skelley/Alamy Stock Photo

My Goals

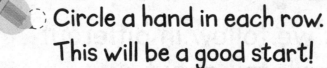 Circle a hand in each row. This will be a good start!

What I Know Now

I can read and understand texts.

I can write about the texts I read.

I know rules we follow in different places.

Key

 I understand.

 I need more practice.

 I do not understand.

 You will come back to the next page later.

Circle a hand in each row. How did you do?

What I Learned

I can read and understand texts.

I can write about the texts I read.

I know rules we follow in different places.

Retell the story.

Write about the story.

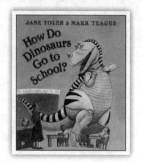

A funny part of the story is

_____

- -

_____

Text Evidence

Page

A part that was not funny is

_____

- -

_____

 Text Evidence

Page

Talk about rules you follow at school.

 Draw and **write** about a rule you follow at school.

A rule is

_____

- -

_____

The **characters** are the people or animals
a fiction story is about.

 Listen to and **look** at pages 14–21.

 Talk about the characters.

 Draw one way the characters act.

Listen to and **look** at pages 24–29.

 Talk about how the characters are acting now.

 Draw one way the characters act.

Rules to Go By   15

Listen to and **look** at pages 14-15.

 Talk about why the author uses capital letters on page 14.

 Write about why the words are shown in this way.

The words are shown in this way because

_____

- -

_____

_____

- -

_____

Listen to and **look** at page 33.
Why do you think the author added
this page?

 Talk about the different dinosaurs
and their names.

 Draw one of the dinosaurs.

Find Text Evidence

Read to find out what the girl can pat.

Circle and read the word **to**.

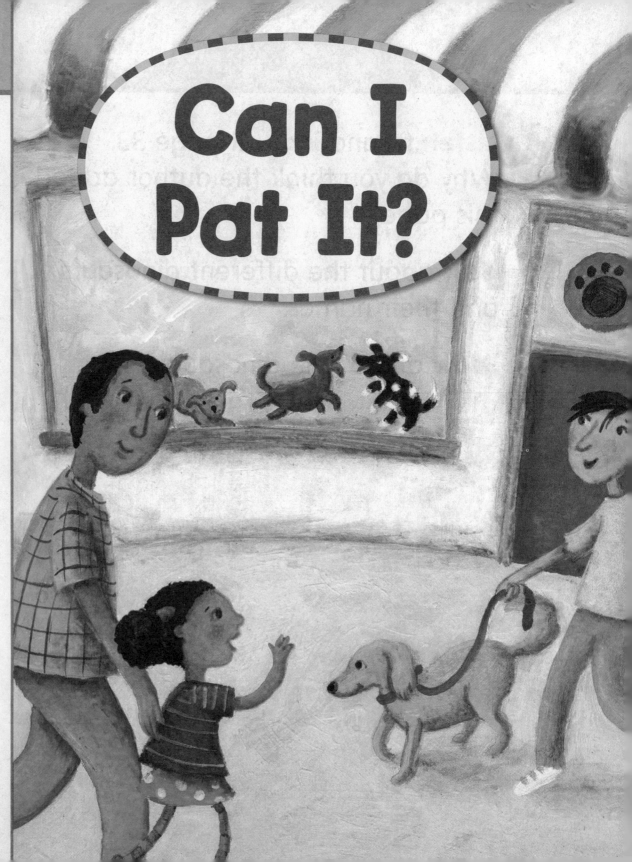

Can I Pat It?

I like to pat it.

Shared Read

🔍 **Find Text Evidence**

✏️ **Underline** the uppercase letters.

✏️ **Circle** what the girl can pat on page 21.

Can I pat it?

I like to pat it.

Shared Read

Find Text Evidence

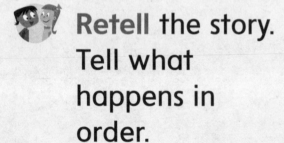 **Circle** an animal whose name has the same middle sound as **pin**.

Retell the story. Tell what happens in order.

I like it.

Can I pat it?

Look at the photo. How can we stay safe when riding a bike?

 Talk about ways the boy stays safe on the bike.

 Circle ways the boy stays safe.

Quick Tip

You can use these sentence starters:

The boy stays safe by ___.

It is not safe to ___.

Comstock/Stockbyte/Getty Images

Listen to the "Biking Rules" list.

 Draw another way you can stay safe on a bike.

 Write the new rule.

Talk About It

How does the author share information about safety?

Shared Read

 **Find Text Evidence**

Read to find out what Tim can tip.

Circle words that have the same middle sound as **sit**.

Tim Can Tip It

Tim can tip the .
pail

Shared Read

 Find Text Evidence

 Circle the word that tells what Tim does with the bag. Use the picture to help you.

 Read and point to each word in the sentence on page 29.

Tim can tip the .

bag

Tim can see the bird tap.

Shared Read

 Find Text Evidence

 Circle and read the word **to**.

 Retell the story. Use the words and pictures to help you.

Tim can see the cat tap.

Tim can sit to pat the .
cat

Rules for Safety

Step 1 Talk about rules we follow for safety.

Step 2 Write a question about how to stay safe at home or school.

_____

- -

_____

_____

- -

_____

Step 3 Look at books or use the Internet.

Step 4 **Draw** and **write** about what you learned.

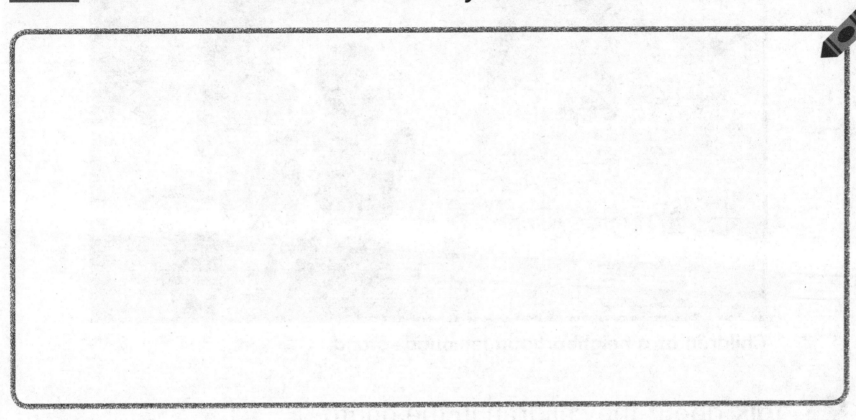

I can stay safe by

_____

- -

_____

Step 5 **Choose** a good way to present your work.

Children at a neighborhood lemonade stand.

 Talk about the children in the photo. What rule are they following?

 Compare these children to the dinosaurs at the end of *How Do Dinosaurs Go to School?*

Quick Tip

You can use these sentence starters:

The children are ___.

This rule is important because ___.

Write a Dinosaur Rule

1 **Think** about the texts you read.
What did you learn about rules
we follow in different places?

2 **Pretend** a dinosaur visits your home.
Draw a picture that shows a rule the
dinosaur should follow.

3 **Write** the rule. Tell why it is important.
Use words that you learned this week.

Think about what you
learned this week.
Turn to page 11.

Build Knowledge

Essential Question What are the different sounds we hear?

Build Vocabulary

 Talk about the different sounds we hear. What words tell about different sounds?

 Draw a picture of one of the words.

Write the word.

A. Chederros/ONOKY/Getty Images

My Goals

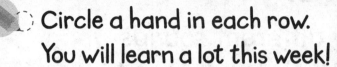 Circle a hand in each row. You will learn a lot this week!

What I Know Now

I can read and understand texts.

I can write about the texts I read.

I know the different sounds we hear.

Key

 I understand.

 I need more practice.

 I do not understand.

 You will come back to the next page later.

Circle a hand in each row. You are doing great!

What I Learned

I can read and understand texts.

I can write about the texts I read.

I know the different sounds we hear.

 Retell the story.

 Write about the story.

A sound the boy hears is

_____

- -

_____

Text Evidence

Page

My favorite sound in the story is

_____

- -

_____

 Text Evidence

Page

Talk about things that make sounds in your neighborhood.

 Draw something that makes a sound.

 Write a sound word for your drawing.

The **setting** is where a fiction story takes place.

 Listen to and **look** at pages 4-5 and pages 22-23.

 Talk about the settings.

 Write about the two settings.

1. _____

2. _____

Draw the settings you wrote about.

1.

2.

Listen to and **look** at pages 20–21 and pages 26–27.

Compare how the sound words look. How do they match the sound?

Write about why the author shows the sound words in this way.

The sound words are big because

_____

- -

_____

The sound words are little because

_____

- -

_____

Listen to and **look** at pages 30–31.

 Talk about who is making the sounds. How do you know?

 Draw who is making the sounds.

Shared Read

 Find Text Evidence

 Read to find out about Nat and Tip.

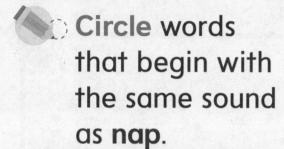 Circle words that begin with the same sound as **nap**.

Nat and Tip

Nat and Tip like the 🎾.

ball

Shared Read

🔍 **Find Text Evidence**

✏️ <u>Underline</u> words that rhyme on page 48.

✏️ **Circle** who Nat and Tip see on page 49.

Nat and Tip like to sip.

Nat and Tip see the  .
children

Shared Read

 Find Text Evidence

Circle and read the word **and**.

Retell the story. Use the words and pictures to help you.

Nat and Tip 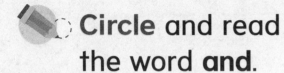 the ___.

hear   hammer

Nat and Tip  the 🐕 !
hear   dog

Look at the photos. How do musical instruments make sounds?

Air makes the trumpet vibrate.

 Circle this musical instrument.

 Draw lines to show sounds coming out of the instrument.

Quick Tip

You can use these sentence starters:

This girl is ____.

The trumpet ____.

Talk about this photo and caption.

 Write what the caption tells about the photo.

Talk About It

How do the photos show ways sounds are being made? What information do the captions add?

Hands beat on the drums and make the drums vibrate.

The caption tells _____

_____

_____

2A Images/Getty Images

 **Find Text Evidence**

Read to find out what Tim and Nan do.

Circle a word that begins with the same sound as **nap**.

Tim and Nan

Arterra Picture Library/Alamy

cluck, cluck

Tim and Nan 👂 the 🐔.
hear   hen

Shared Read

🔍 **Find Text Evidence**

✏️ **Circle** an object whose name ends with the same sound as **sun**.

✏️ **Underline** and read the word **and**.

Tim and Nan 👂 the 🚜.

hear   tractor

Jupiterimages/Photolibrary/Getty Images

Tim and Nan see the  .

corn

Shared Read

🔍 **Find Text Evidence**

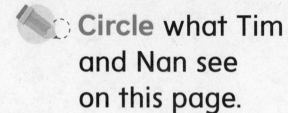 **Circle** what Tim and Nan see on this page.

 **Retell** the text. Use the words and photos to help you.

Tim and Nan see the 🏠.

barn

Richard Price/Photographer's Choice/Getty Images

Tim and Nan the .

hear · pig

Experiment with Sounds

Step 1 Talk about objects that you might use to make sounds. Choose some to try.

Step 2 Write a question about sounds you might make with your objects.

_____

- -

_____

_____

- -

_____

Step 3 Experiment with your objects. Try different ways to make sounds.

Step 4 Draw how you made sounds with your objects. **Label** your picture with a sound word.

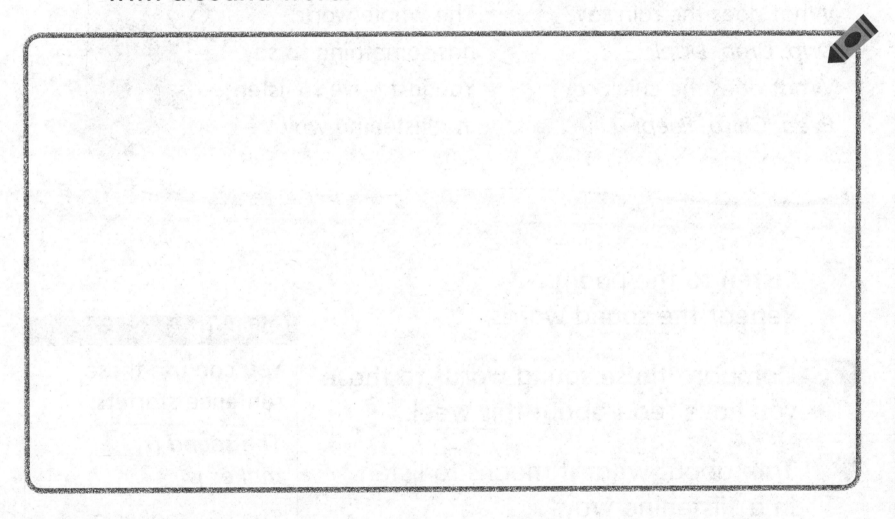

Step 5 Choose a good way to present your work.

What Does the Rain Say?

What does the rain say?

Drip, Drop, Drip!

What does the chick say?

Peep, Chirp, Peep!

The whole world

has something to say.

You just have to listen

in a listening way.

 Listen to the poem.
Repeat the sound words.

 Compare these sound words to those you have read about this week.

 Talk about what it means to listen in a "listening way."

Quick Tip

You can use these sentence starters:

The sound a ___ makes is ___.

The ___ makes a ___ sound.

Write a Riddle

1 **Think** about the texts you read. What did you learn about the different sounds we hear?

2 **Choose** a favorite sound you read about. **Draw** what makes the sound.

3 **Write** a riddle about what makes the sound. Use words that you learned this week.

Think about what you learned this week.
Turn to page 39.

Build Knowledge

? Essential Question What places do you go to during the week?

Build Vocabulary

 Talk about places you go to during the week. What are some words that name these places?

 Draw a picture of one of the places.

 Write the word.

My Goals

Circle a hand in each row. There are no wrong answers!

What I Know Now

I can read and understand texts.

I can write about the texts I read.

I know places I go to during the week.

Key

 I understand.

 I need more practice.

 I do not understand.

 You will come back to the next page later.

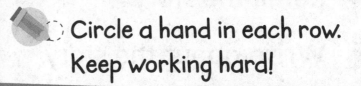
What I Learned

I can read and understand texts.

I can write about the texts I read.

I know places I go to during the week.

Retell the story.

 Write about the story.

The setting of this story is

_____

- -

_____

Text Evidence

Page

An interesting place the dog goes is

_____

- -

_____

_____

- -

_____

Text Evidence

Page

Talk about where you would take a pet in your neighborhood.

 Draw and **write** about this place.

I would take a pet to

_____

- -

_____

The main character is the person or animal a fiction story is mostly about.

 Listen to the story.

 Talk about the main character.

 Write about the main character.

The main character

_____

- - - - - - - - - - - - - - - - - - -

_____

_____

- - - - - - - - - - - - - - - - - - -

_____

Draw the main character and a detail about this character.

Listen to and **look** at pages 6-8.

 Talk about who is telling the story. What does this character need to do?

 Draw and **write** about what this character needs to do.

I need to

_____

- -

_____

Listen to and **look** at pages 14-16.

 Talk about why the character wants to say hello. How does the illustrator show this?

 Draw what the illustrator shows.

🔍 **Find Text Evidence**

💭 Read to find out about the visit to see Nan.

✏️ **Circle** and read the word **go**.

We Go to See Nan

Cam and I go to see Nan.

Find Text Evidence

 Underline words that begin with the same sound as **cap**.

 Circle words that rhyme on this page.

Cam can pat the cat.

We can see the .

book

Shared Read

Find Text Evidence

Circle who can sit on pages 78–79.

Retell the story. Use the words and pictures to help you.

Cam can go and sit.

The cat and I go and sit.

Look at the map and the map key. How can these tools help us to learn about neighborhood places?

 Talk about the pictures in the map key.

 Draw a line from each picture on the map key to the place on the map.

Quick Tip

You can say:

The map shows ____.

The map key shows ____.

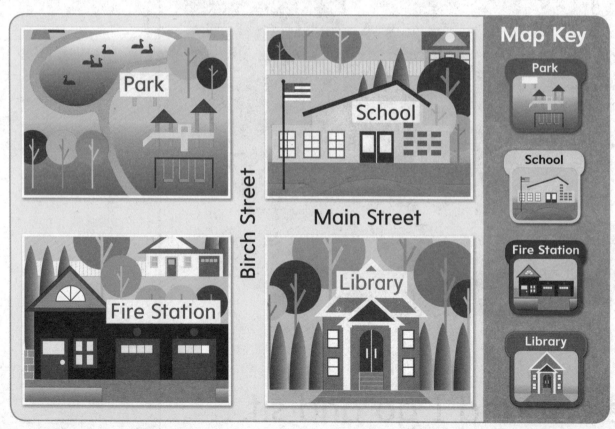

Talk about the places on the map.

 Draw and **write** about what people do in one of the places.

Talk About It

What does the map tell you about the neighborhood? How does the map key help you to use the map?

Can We Go?

Read to find out where the girl and her mom can go.

Think about what they can do at the library. Make a picture in your mind.

Can we go to the ?
library

Shared Read

 Find Text Evidence

 Underline words that begin with the same sound as **cap**.

 Circle how the girl and her mom can go to the library.

We can go in a .

taxi

Glow Images, Inc/Getty Images

Can we go to the market?

Shared Read

 **Find Text Evidence**

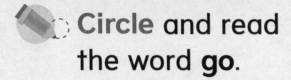 **Circle** and read the word **go**.

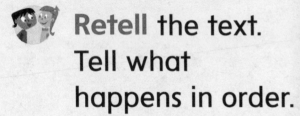 **Retell** the text. Tell what happens in order.

We can go in a .

bus

We can go, go, go!

Research and Inquiry

School Places Interview

Step 1 Talk about the places in your school.
Choose one place to learn about.

Step 2 Write a question about this place.

_____

- -

_____

_____

- -

_____

Step 3 Visit the place you picked.
Ask the people there your question.

Step 4 Draw and write about what you learned.

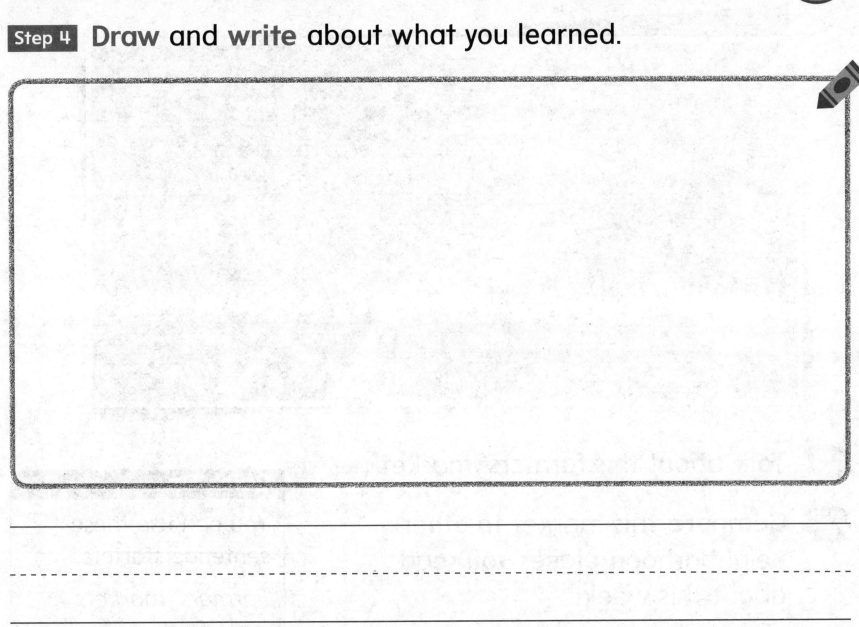

Step 5 Choose a good way to present your work.

 Talk about this farmers' market.

 Compare this market to other neighborhood places you read about this week.

Quick Tip

You can use these sentence starters:

Farmers' markets have fresh ___.

We can buy ___.

Write About Your Neighborhood

1 **Think** about the texts you read.
What did you learn about places
you go to during the week?

2 **Draw** a place in your neighborhood.
How is it like a place from the texts?
How is it different?

3 **Write** how the place is alike and
different. Use words that you learned
this week.

Think about what you
learned this week.
Turn to page 67.

Think About Your Learning

Think about what you learned in this unit.

 Share one thing you did well.

 Write one thing you want to get better at.

_____

- -

_____

- -

_____

Share a goal you have with your partner.

My Sound-Spellings

Aa
a
apple

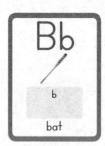

Bb
b
bat

Cc
c ck k
camel

Dd
d
dolphin

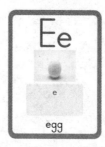

Ee
e
egg

Ff
f
fire

Gg
g
guitar

Hh
h_
hippo

Ii
i
insect

Jj
j
jump

Kk
c k ck
koala

Ll
l
lemon

Mm
m
map

Nn
n
nest

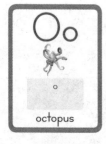

Oo
o
octopus

Pp
p
piano

Qq
qu_
queen

Rr
r
rose

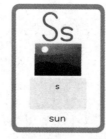

Ss
s
sun

Tt
t
turtle

Uu
u
umbrella

Vv
v
volcano

Ww
w_
window

Xx
x
box

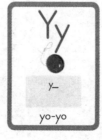

Yy
y_
yo-yo

Zz
z
_s
zipper

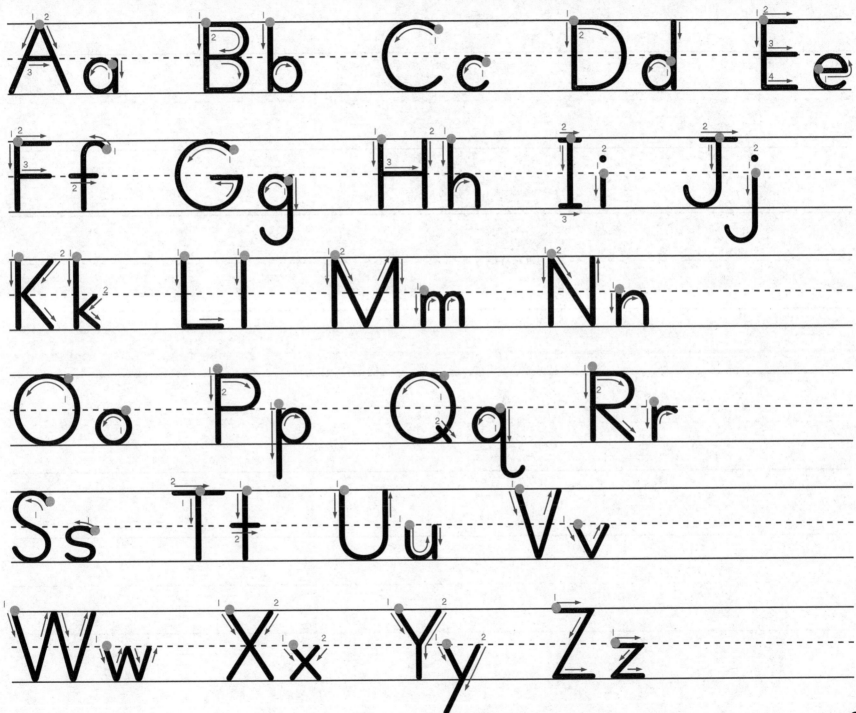